This book belongs to:

Kay Yost

JUMP BALL

BOOKS BY MEL GLENN

Poetry

The Taking of Room 114

Who Killed Mr. Chippendale?

Class Dismissed

Class Dismissed II

Back to Class

My Friend's Got This Problem, Mr. Candler

Novels

One Order to Go

Play-By-Play

Squeeze Play

MEL GLENN

A BASKETBALL
SEASON IN POEMS

LODESTAR BOOKS

Dutton
New York

Library of Congress Cataloging-in-Publication Data

Glenn, Mel.
Jump ball: a basketball season in poems / Mel Glenn.—1st ed.
p. cm.
Summary: Tells the story of a high school basketball team's season through a series
of poems reflecting the feelings of students, their families, teachers, and coaches.
ISBN 0-525-67554-X (alk. paper)
1. Basketball teams—Poetry.   2. High school students—Poetry.
3. Young adult poetry—American. [1. Basketball—Poetry.
2. High schools—Poetry.   3. Schools—Poetry.   4. American poetry.]
I. Title.
PS3557.L447J86   1997
811'.54—dc21
97-9902   CIP   AC

Published in the United States by Lodestar Books,
an affiliate of Dutton Children's Books,
a member of Penguin Putnam Inc.,
375 Hudson Street, New York, New York 10014

Published simultaneously in Canada
by McClelland & Stewart, Toronto

Editor: Rosemary Brosnan   Designer: Barbara Powderly
Printed in the U.S.A.   First Edition   10 9 8 7 6 5 4 3 2 1

for Elyse, my wife,
a non-sports fan
who liked the book anyway

PROLOGUE

Jeffrey Townsend, Weatherman

THIS IS JEFFREY TOWNSEND FROM THE NATIONAL WEATHER SERVICE, HERE IN WASHINGTON, D.C., WHERE A WINTER STORM WATCH IS IN EFFECT FOR THE EASTERN HALF OF THE COUNTRY. ALREADY, SNOW HAS BLASTED THROUGH MONTANA AND THE PLAINS STATES. NORTH AND SOUTH DAKOTA HAVE BEEN PARTICULARLY HARD HIT. IN FARGO, NORTH DAKOTA, DRIFTS HAVE REACHED FIVE FEET. AND AS YOU CAN TELL FROM THE LATEST SATELLITE PICTURES, DRIVING IS EXTREMELY HAZARDOUS, IF NOT IMPOSSIBLE. DRIVERS ARE WARNED TO STAY OFF THE ROADS. IN NEBRASKA, THREE PEOPLE WERE KILLED WHEN THEIR CAMPER SLID OFF THE ROAD AND TUMBLED INTO AN ICY RAVINE. WE WILL CONTINUE TO TRACK THIS STORM AS IT HEADS EAST . . .

FIRST QUARTER: TRYOUTS

5, 4, 3, 2, 1—Cue Tim

THIS IS TIM McHALE, REPORTING FOR SPORTSCABLE 3. TONIGHT, WE ARE GOING TO PRESENT THE FIRST IN OUR SERIES OF PRESEASON BASKETBALL SHOWS. TONIGHT, WE WILL HIGHLIGHT THE TIGERS OF TOWER HIGH. YOU'LL MEET THE PLAYERS AND THE COACH, HEAR FROM THE PARENTS AND THE FANS, AND LISTEN TO SOME PEOPLE WHO BELIEVE THAT BASKETBALL IS DRIVING AMERICAN TEENAGERS DOWN THE WRONG LANE. ALL EYES ARE ON THE TIGERS THIS YEAR, AND ESPECIALLY ON THEIR CONSENSUS ALL-AMERICAN, GARRETT JAMES, THE EXCITING AND ELECTRIFYING POINT GUARD WHO BRINGS THE CROWD TO ITS FEET WITH HIS MAGICAL SPIN MOVES AND PRECISION PASSING. SO JOIN US AS WE PRESENT THE SIGHTS AND SOUNDS OF TIGER BASKETBALL.

Tiger, tiger, burning bright,
On the gym floor every night.
Rock 'em,
Sock 'em,
Kill 'em,
Knock 'em.
Tiger, tiger, burning bright,
On the gym floor every night.
Rip 'em,
Zip 'em,
Beat 'em,
Flip 'em.
What immortal hand or eye
Could follow the ball as it flies.
Tiger, tiger, burning bright
On the gym floor every night.

Greg Hoskins, Coach

We're family.

We practice harder than anyone.

We play together as a team.

There are no prima donnas here.

The team has lots of character, lots of heart.

We will play one game at a time.

We will be in the thick of it.

The rest of the league is real strong.

We hope to step up in big situations.

Come on, guys, gimme a break.

The season ain't even started yet.

How many clichés do you writers want?

Why don't you ask me some intelligent questions.

James?

He's just another member of the team.

Yeah, I'm serious.

Sharif Daniels, Student Fan

Screw school.
What does he need it for?
What they gonna teach him?
How to do
Research on the history of the game?
How to figure out
The air pressure needed to pump up a basketball?
Get outta here.
He could hook up with an NBA team right now.
I ain't lyin' to you, he could.
He should take the money and run,
Run up and down the floor
Of every pro court in America.
Hey, don't you guys wanna talk to me?
I could tell you all about my man, James.

Nathan Scribner, English Teacher

That's right,
Garrett James is in my English class,
Third row, second seat.
Would you gentlemen be interviewing me
If I had the best writer here in my class?
Would you care if Garrett could
Sink a series of sonnets,
Throw up a few terza rimas,
Pass around a bouquet of pastoral poems,
Drive down the lane with a poetic license?
I don't think so.
I'm more excited if he can
Understand the complexities of a play,
Instead of the complexities of a trapping defense,
Diagram a sentence,
Instead of an inbounds play,
Shoot for a career after basketball,
Instead of one in it.
But what do I know?
I'm only his English teacher.
He doesn't need me.
He needs only a good agent,
Who speaks the language of money.

George Paley, History Teacher

You're the reporter from the cable station, right?
You're interviewing me because
I'm the oldest teacher here?
I'm not so sure I'm flattered, Mr. McHale, is it?
My opinion of Garrett James, the basketball player?
I'm sure he's a nice young man,
But I decry the circuslike atmosphere surrounding him.
It is harmful for our school
Because it promotes elitism based on false values.
Because a boy can throw a ball
Of a certain circumference
Into a hoop with a slightly larger circumference,
I should be expected to stand up and cheer?
Call me an old grouch if you want to,
But I believe that the straightest path to knowledge
Still lies on the line of hard work and study.
It cannot be found on the arc of a basketball.
I have seen people at these contests
Wildly pounding the air with their fists
In exultation or derision.
What a shocking waste of mental energy.
Academics are far more important than sports,
Hands down.

Garrett James

No, I don't know which scouts are here.
No, I don't know which college I'll attend.
No, I don't know which defense our team will use.
No, I don't know which sneakers I'll wear.
Speak to my coach.
No, I don't know when I can talk to you.
No, I don't know when I can do the interview.
No, I don't know when I can miss class.
No, I don't know when I can sign the photos.
Speak to my principal.
No, I don't have a favorite color.
No, I don't have a favorite food.
No, I don't have a favorite girl.
No, I don't have a favorite pro team.
Speak to my mother.
Yeah, I can speak for myself.
I do my talkin' on the court.

oretta James

With one older brother who plays basketball
And one younger sister who sings in the church choir,
I am caught in the middle.
My big brother gets all the headlines.
My little sister gets all the applause.
I feed myself on the pages of my diary,
And in it I pour out all my hatred,
By writing vicious descriptions of everyone I know,
Especially my soon-to-be very famous brother.
You think it's such a joy living with him?
I could really tell you some good stuff.
When my mother found my diary,
She freaked over
The items of injury,
The sentences of scorn
I had written oh, so neatly.
"What's this?" she said, confused.
I didn't even answer her.
I left the room knowing
That for one glorious moment
I was the shooting star.

Aaron Loudermilk,
Hudson Landing Teen

Man, it's dead around here.
Ain't nothin' happenin'.
Nearest movie is ten miles away,
Nearest mall is five.
Can't get there anyway—
My pickup ain't pickin' up.
You wanna shoot some hoops
Down in the church basement?
Me, neither.
Shit, it's cold.
I hear we're gonna get more snow.
You got a joint?
Me, neither.
We could go to the mini-mart
And pick up a six-pack.
You got some change?
Me, neither.
Hey, you hear that?
Sounded like a crash.
You wanna go check it out?
Me, neither.
Man, it's dead around here.

Flora James

You ain't such a star
    You can't pick up your room,
    You can't get me my medicine,
    You can't watch your sister.
You ain't such a star
    You can't go to church,
    You can't visit your grandma,
    You can't do the laundry.
One day your talent may take us outta here,
    Outta broken elevators and windows,
    Outta cracked plaster and crack heads,
    Outta abandoned buildings and abandoned lives.
But until that day, my child,
You still my little boy,
And I put too much effort
Into raisin' you right
For me to see it go to waste.
The whole world may be impressed with you,
But you ain't impressin' me none
Until you do your chores,
Until you do God's work
And your own.
You hear me, son?

Howie Grunwald

Hey, kid, you wanna play some b-ball?
You've got a sweet move to the basket.
I can hook you up with Coach Hoskins right now.
He's a real good friend of mine.
You're what, 6'2", 185?
Still growing, I bet.
Look, I can guarantee you you'll start,
If I am any judge of talent.
James will be gone by then and
You'll get all the floor time you desire.
Hey, what number you want?
Jordan's?
I can get it for you.
What grade you in?
Eighth?
No doubt about it.
You're gonna be a star at
Tower High School next year.
Just stick with me, kid.

Dennis Carleton

When I was five,
My father put up a basketball hoop
On a telephone pole outside our apartment.
I practiced hard to be my father's son,
But all I learned was
Asphalt shimmers in the summer heat
And fingers sting in the winter's half light.
I know I am not good enough
To play varsity ball, but
My father insists I try out for the Tigers anyway.
I know my shots will miss
Even before they fall off the rim.
I know I'll be cut
Even before the coach calls, "Next!"
Somewhere,
Between the ball and the backboard,
Between the paint and the perimeter,
I know I'll let my father down.
What happens to a dream
Deflated?

⬤Jason Cohen

"On the line shooting a pair, Jason Cohen.
The game is literally in his hands.
No time left on the clock.
It has come down to this:
He hits one and we go into overtime,
Two, and the Tigers win.
Back to you, Bob."

"Cohen bounces the ball once, twice.
It's up . . . Tie score!
The crowd is going wild.
Cohen takes a deep breath,
The ball is up and it's
Gooood! Tigers win, Tigers win."

"Hey, Cohen, get off the line.
Tryouts aren't for another hour.
You wanna do me a favor?
Go down to the locker room and
Pick up the water bottles.
The regulars will need 'em."

"Yes, Coach."

Rebecca Rosenfelder

My sister, Rachel, who's twenty-six and is
Living in a basement apartment
Comes home for Sabbath dinners.
She's a drug counselor
For elementary schools.
She tells me about the fourth graders who smoke pot
And the sixth graders who are into cocaine.
She also tells me there are no men around for her.
Most of the guys she meets are
Divorced, gay, or married,
Or what is worse, not Jewish.
Most of the guys she meets are pigs.
"I'm not holding out for Prince Charming," she says,
"I'd settle for just charming.
Anyway, how's school, kiddo?"
I start to complain about teachers and tests
And about my boyfriend, Jason,
Who talks only about basketball.
"I wish I were back in high school," she says,
Taking the leftovers back to her basement apartment.

Tamba Senesie

In Nigeria,
My father is a university professor.
Everyone knows his name.
When he walks down the streets of our village,
Everyone tips their hats to him.
The little children pull at his leg.
The market women give him free oranges.
The old pas ask him many questions.
In America,
My father is a visiting university professor.
Nobody knows his name.
When he walks down the streets of the city,
Everyone pushes their way past him.
But my father does not seem to mind.
He walks like a man who knows who he is.
I will never be as distinguished as my father.
I do not possess his intellectual gifts.
But my tall body and broad shoulders
Give me confidence on the basketball court.
Soon,
With much work and Allah's blessing,
Everybody will know my name,
In this country.

Steven Walker

First,
My neighbor's neighbor gets shot,
No big deal.
Then,
My neighbor gets shot,
Nothin' serious.
Then,
My cousin's cousin gets shot,
Just nicked him.
Then,
My cousin gets shot,
Just scratched his skin.
Then,
My friend's friend gets shot,
Hardly knew him.
Then,
My friend gets shot,
Known him all my life.
Hey, this is getting too close, man.
All I want to do is finish school
And maybe try out for the basketball team.
That is, if I don't get shot,
First.

Daisy Mejías

My boyfriend, Steven,
Talks in a language I don't understand:
Points in the paint,
Post up down low,
Pull up for a trey.
I talk to him in another language:
Shop 'til I drop,
Get my nails wrapped,
Look for the right top.
He wants to try out for the basketball team.
I want him to go to the mall with me.
He wants to check out the sports bar.
I want to check out the cosmetics bar.
He wants to sharpen his shooting eye.
I want to sharpen my eye for bargains.
It's OK we don't talk to each other all that much.
There are other ways to communicate.
And when we're finished doing that
We're too tired to speak
In any language at all.

William Flanders, Motorist

I know the road's icy, Carol.
I'm going slow, stop nagging.
Why should I hurry to get to their house?
For a piece of burnt chicken?
I still don't like him, never have.
Why our daughter married him, I don't know.
What kind of job is that for a married man?
Merchant marine—he's away more than he's home.
Is that good for our grandson?
Why'd they move way up here?
Hudson Landing—who ever heard of it?
Yeah, yeah, I see the bus behind me.
In the rearview mirror, what do you think?
Yeah, I'm letting him pass me.
What's his hurry?
Probably a piece of burnt chicken.
He's all over the road, my God,
He's going off the road, he's flipping over.
Get me my cellular, in the glove compartment!
QUICK! Dial 911.
Oh my God!

E. Z. Pratt

My girlfriend says I'm the father.
Hey, man, I ain't got time for that.
I got too many things to do.
I gotta get my stuff together.
Pass a few classes to be eligible,
Then make the team,
Be a crazy star,
So that the colleges will come after me,
Offerin' me this,
Givin' me that.
She tryin' to pin this on me?
What she goin' and sayin' that for?
That kid of hers has too many fathers.
Havin' a family just ain't for me, man,
Poop and Pampers and all that.
I ain't havin' none of it.
The only one I'm takin' care of is
Me.

P. J. Pratt

My girlfriend says I'm the father?
Hey, man, I got lots of time for that.
I got nothin' else to do.
I got my stuff together.
I'm passin' all my classes.
Makin' the grades,
Bein' the nerd,
So that colleges will come after me,
Offerin' me this,
Givin' me that.
She sayin' it ain't mine?
What she goin' and sayin' that for?
Shit, I'm the only one's been with her.
Havin' a family is just what I need, man,
Poop and Pampers and all that.
I'm havin' all of it.
The only ones I'm takin' care of is
Me . . . and my family.

uliette Paris

"You got involved with the wrong brother,"
My parents protest.
"Why'd you get mixed up with E.Z. instead of P.J.?"
My sisters scream.
Why did I?
P.J. is reliable.
He got a job.
P.J. is sweet.
He brings his girl flowers for no reason.
P.J. knows how to treat a lady.
He interested in more than just screwin'.
E.Z. is unreliable.
He ain't even lookin' for work.
E.Z. is nasty.
He brings me nothin' but grief.
E.Z. don't know the first thing 'bout treatin' a lady.
He only interested in sleepin' with me.
Everybody tells me I'm a fool to stay with E.Z.,
But he's the father of my child,
And I ain't about to trade one brother for another.
I love E.Z., no matter what my parents and sisters say.
They don't know shit about love, none of 'em.
Who's to say what love is.
It's a relative thing, I guess.

Tysheen Stanton

The way I look at things is
You have to shoot for a goal,
Figuratively.
You have to run around,
Or through your opponent,
Literally.
You have to
Stand tall,
Move fast,
Play hard,
While everyone on the sidelines is
Looking at your every move.
You have to grab the ball,
Or the world,
With two hands
And jam that sucker home.
You watch me today at the tryouts.
I'm ready to step up to a whole new level.
Basketball is my life.
It's the only game in town.
It's the only thing I know.

Darius Stanton, Father

I take my boy fishing and he tells me
He's gonna be a pro ballplayer.
"I got all the slick moves," he says.
Off the court he ain't so slick.
"What you gonna do while
You waiting for the draft?" I ask.
"I don't know," he says, baiting another hook.
I try to tell him in real life
You gotta get up every morning.
You gotta get to work on time.
You gotta do your job.
He laughs and tells me to chill.
"Dad, I'm gonna retire you,
Buy you a big boat so
You can go fishing all the time."
Yeah, right.
When's he gonna realize
He ain't never gonna get
A nibble from any team out there.
He ain't never gonna catch
Anything more than scale pay,
Just like me.

arnell Joyce

The home and away games of my life
Bounce from one crazy arena to another.

Home			Away	
No heat			Plenty of heat	
In my apartment	(0)		In my classroom	(2)
Mom didn't			Free breakfast	
Buy no food	(0)		In cafeteria	(2)
Dad disappeared			Teachers there	
Last year	(0)		Every day	(2)
Neighborhood run			School run	
By drug addicts	(0)		By principal	(2)
Local park			School gym	
Messed up	(0)		In perfect shape	(2)

Final Score
Away 10 points
Home 0 points

Game Summary
No home court advantage
Workin' here.
Time to get this show on the road
And climb up outta bed.

Parnell Payne

I'm a sweet-walkin',
  trash-talkin',
  guard-stalkin'
  mano on the court.
I'm a lane-drivin',
  high-fivin',
  ball-divin'
  big bro on the court.
I'm a head-bangin',
  rim-hangin',
  bell-clangin'
  all-go on the court.
I'm a cool-rappin',
  ball tap-in,
  no-nappin'
  star pro on the court.

Parnell's my name,
You got no game.
Listen up, fool,
I'm takin' you to school.

⬤yrone Porter

Coach,
What do you mean
I gotta go for more tests?
There ain't nothin' wrong with me.
See the note the doc give me?
It says I'm all right.
Yeah, I know he wants me to take more tests.
I'll do it—after the season.
Yeah, I know I got a few extra beats.
So what? No big thing, I'm musical, Coach.
Yeah, I know I'm being a smart-ass.
Look, you gotta let me play ball.
I'm as strong as a bull,
Maybe even a Chicago Bull.
OK, OK, I'll go for the test,
But it's a waste of time, I tell ya.
You gotta know
That if I don't play ball,
It will break my heart.
Then we won't have to worry about no test,
Will we, Coach?

Janice Crosby, County Dispatch

This is Central Dispatch for Saratoga County.
What is the nature of the emergency?
Please calm down, sir.
What is your name?
Mr. Flanders, please calm down and
Tell me what happened.
What bus?
What road?
What embankment?
Where are you, sir?
North of Saratoga Springs, on 9?
How far?
No, don't go down the hill, stay put.
We'll be right there.
Hold for a second, sir.
      Maxine, call the state troopers,
      Tell them we have
      A serious motor vehicle accident,
      Three miles south of Hudson Landing.
      Notify fire and emergency units, too.
Mr. Flanders, Mr. Flanders,
Are you still there?
What can you see?

Nestor Padilla

Just because I come from Ponce in P.R.
Does not mean I do not know
How to play basketball.
Just because I grew up with football
(You call it soccer)
Does not mean I am ignorant of the game.
I am a true athlete in any sport.
Sí, baseball was my favorite activity.
I would stand in the hot sun for hours,
Waiting in the outfield for them
To try and hit the ball past me.
It rarely happened.
I caught the ball so many times
The opposing team was always amazed.
But in America, to fit in,
To be one of the guys, as they say,
You must learn
The politics of the playground,
The rhythm of the rim,
And the sweet swoosh
Of the ball hitting nothing but net.

⬤oman Kirenova

Just because I come from Kiev in Ukraine,
Does not mean I do not know
How to play basketball.
Just because I grew up with football
(You call it soccer)
Does not mean I am ignorant of game.
I am true athlete in any sport.
Da, ice hockey was my favorite activity.
I would crouch in cold wind for hours,
Waiting in goal crease for them
To try and slap puck past me.
It rarely happened.
I caught puck so many times
The opposing team was always amazed.
But in America, to fit in,
To be one of guys, as they say,
You must learn
Politics of the playground,
Rhythm of the rim,
And sweet swoosh
Of ball hitting nothing but net.

Vonessa Leighton, Team Manager

Mighty pecs,
Muscled necks,
Amazing biceps,
Flashy triceps.
Taking tabs
On super abs,
Zero fat's
Where I'm at.
Rounded buns,
Lots of fun,
Sweaty skin
For the mood I'm in.
Six foot nine,
God, so fine,
Gorgeous hunks,
Ain't no punks.
Got the best of all jobs, it seems,
Manager of the Tigers basketball team.

Valdeen DeForest

My mother wanted to be a doctor;
She was told to be a nurse.
My aunt wanted to be a pilot;
She was told to be a flight attendant.
My cousin wanted to be a sportscaster;
She was told to be an executive assistant.
What is going on here?
I thought the battles had been fought,
The war had been won
So I could be anything I want.
I *am* what I want to be—
Captain of the girls' volleyball team.
But we girls still live the segregated sports life
In the separate spheres of apartheid athletics.
The boys get the better
Equipment, gyms, and budgets,
And double the number of articles in the school paper.
Our situation will not change
If the boys' basketball team gets all the publicity
While the girls are told we are just
Too cute for words.

Darnell Joyce

The only thing I ever wanted
Was to play Tiger basketball,
To wear the orange and black,
To hear the roar of the crowd,
To smell the hardwood floor.
On the walls of my side of the room
Are posters of stars, past and present:
Dr. J., Magic, Kareem, Bird,
Shaq, Michael, Penny, and Patrick.
A draft is not from an open window.
A bucket is not a large pail.
A foul is not a chicken and
A jam is not a jelly.
I made the cut!
I made the team!
I can wear the jersey!
I'm gonna have to put up some more posters
And stare at the crowded wall,
Knowing the game clock of my life
Has just started.

Parnell Payne

The only thing I ever wanted
Was to play Tiger basketball,
To wear the orange and black,
To hear the roar of the crowd,
To smell the hardwood floor.
On the walls of my room
Are posters of stars, past and present:
Reed, Bradley, West, Monroe,
Sir Charles, David, Karl, and Alonzo.
A draft is only from an open window.
A bucket is only a large pail.
A fowl is only a chicken and
A jam is only a jelly.
I didn't make the cut.
I didn't make the team.
I can never wear the jersey.
I'm gonna have to tear down all my posters
And stare at the blank wall,
Knowing that the game clock of my life
Has just ended.

Tony Grimaldi

For thirty years I carried the mail,
Delivering letters that connected people,
Until my sciatica forced me
To transfer to the local office,
Where I sorted the mail in the back room.
I never married;
My mother was sick and I was
The only one left to care for her.
When she died, the silence in the house
Nearly drove me crazy.
The empty rooms forced me
Out into the neighborhood,
And I found myself
Back at the old high school,
Attending varsity games of all kinds.
How I marveled at the athletes I saw.
I began to help the teams out with
Carfare, candy, and advice,
And the smiles of appreciation I received
Lifted me out of my loneliness,
Connected me to people again.
I give my stamp of approval
To these wonderful youngsters.
They are all
First-class.

SECOND QUARTER: THE SEASON

5, 4, 3, 2, 1—Cue Tim

THIS IS TIM McHALE, REPORTING FOR SPORTSCABLE 3.
WE ARE COMING TO YOU FROM THE TIGERS' GYM,
WHERE, IN A MATTER OF MOMENTS, GARRETT JAMES,
THE CONSENSUS ALL-AMERICAN, WILL LEAD HIS
POWER-PACKED TEAM AGAINST THE EAGLES OF
EISENHOWER HIGH IN THE FIRST GAME OF THE SEASON.
COACH HOSKINS, CAN WE GET A WORD WITH YOU?

HOW DO THE PLAYERS FEEL? NERVOUS, I BET. HOW
DO YOU MATCH UP AGAINST EISENHOWER HIGH? EVEN
UP, I'M SURE. HOW MANY POINTS WILL JAMES SCORE?
THIRTY, AT LEAST. DO YOU THINK YOU CAN GO
UNDEFEATED? A DEFINITE POSSIBILITY. DO YOU THINK
YOUR BENCH IS STRONG? YOU'VE GOT THE HORSES.
DO YOU THINK JAMES WILL BREAK ALL SCORING
RECORDS? NO DOUBT.

WE REALLY WANT TO HEAR WHAT YOU HAVE TO
SAY—RIGHT AFTER THIS COMMERCIAL BREAK.

Tower Tigers Cheer

Tiger, tiger, burning bright,
Ain't our team just outta sight?
Raining, draining,
Twos and threes,
Get that loose ball
On your knees.
Tiger, tiger, burning bright,
Ain't our team just outta sight?
Driving, diving
Toward the hoop,
Throw that lead pass,
Alley-oop.
No immortal hand or eye,
It's Tower High School, do or die.
Tiger, tiger, burning bright,
Ain't our team just outta sight?

Lloyd Wallace, Tower Parent

They'll send the limo for him.
They'll send the plane.
They'll take him to the best restaurant in town,
And they'll tell him
That whatever he wants he can definitely have.
He will get a full scholarship.
He will get his choice of dorms.
He will get his own private tutor.
My boy?
They sent him a postcard.
They sent him a map of the city.
They gave him a meal ticket to the school cafeteria.
And they told him
That whatever he wanted he could probably get.
He might be eligible for financial aid.
He might be able to get the dorm of his choice.
He might not be closed out of too many classes.
Am I bitter?
What do you think?
Hey, but that's life.
I'll tell you one thing, though.
I wish my boy was born
With a basketball in his hand,
Rather than a brain in his head.

Fiona Sullivan, Physics Teacher

To all my old-fogy colleagues,
Who seem to think that
Basketball has assumed some
Inordinate celestial weight
In the educational firmament,
I have a simple message: "Get a life!"
I'd also like to present to you
A position paper, actually five positions—
Two guards, two forwards, and a center.
As a die-hard Celtics fan, I can surely say
Basketball is a Boston ballet
With its own intricate steps and patterns.
As a die-hard Tigers fan, I can surely say
Basketball is a never-boring minidrama
With its final outcome unscripted.
For all my colleagues who travel
On the high road of snobbery,
Let me tell you to get
Down and dirty in the low post
And watch with wonderment
As bodies in motion
Whip unerring passes
Within prescribed cosmic borders,
According to the harmonious laws
Of Newton and Naismith.

Mary Beth Hoskins

In high school,
On our first date,
My future husband
Took me to a basketball game.
In college,
On our umpteenth date,
My husband-to-be
Proposed to me at halftime.
For our honeymoon,
On the first day of spring,
My new husband
Wanted to go to the Basketball Hall of Fame.
For my birthday,
On the first day of winter,
My darling husband
Bought two tickets to the NBA All-Star game.
The man eats, sleeps, and lives basketball.
I often eat, sleep, and live alone.
But I don't mind all that much.
A man with a passion is better than
A man with no passion at all.
What has held me close these years is
That our relationship is as intense
As the last minute of any closely contested game.
My life with Greg has been a ball,
A basketball, one that bounces straight and true.

Greg Hoskins, Coach

OK, guys, listen up.
Before we start our season,
We're going to take a team picture.
But before we line up for that,
I want to remind you of a few rules:
You miss practice or, God forbid, a game,
You better be bleeding.
You miss classes,
You better make them up.
You miss your exams,
You better have a good excuse.
You get in trouble on the outside,
You better move to another state.
You disrespect anybody, *anybody,*
You better get used to the bench.
You talk back to me,
You better turn in your uniform.
You guys got that?
Good.
Cohen, get the photographer over here,
We're ready.
Anybody can't follow these rules?
You're out of the picture.

Tysheen Stanton

OK, OK, I know it's only one game.
You think I'm nervous?
No way, man.
Just because
My father's in the house,
My brother's in the house,
My girlfriend's in the house,
The whole world is in the house?
Well, maybe a bit.
But if you watch me,
I'm ready to step up to a whole new level.
I got my granny down in South Carolina
Saying some powerful prayers for me.
Truth?
I hope I don't pee in my pants
Before the opening tip.
I'm going to try my best.
I've got to show my father
James isn't the only one
Grabbing the ball
And the headlines tonight.

Jason Cohen

Last year, before the first game,
When I had failed two subjects and
Wasn't allowed to play any ball,
I got screamed at by every adult I knew.
Everybody, except my grandma,
Ganged up on me and yelled
I would have to pass my classes,
Instead of the ball,
That I would have to hit the books,
Instead of the boards.
This year, before the first game,
I am copacetic with English—
You like that fancy word?
I am up to date in history—
Note my interest in current events.
I am square with geometry—
A little math humor there.
I am *bon* with French—
Ah, *naturellement, mon ami.*
And I am taking the measure of chemistry—
Bonding with the subject, I might add.
Working hard on and off the court
Is the only way I know
To make the grade.

Jolene Hanks, Cashier, Hudson Hardware

You hear the fire bell, Fran?
Probably just a false alarm.
You know, the McGrory twins again.
Just because their father's the fire chief,
They like to fool around with that bell.
Makes their papa look bad, don't it?
Guess all the kids around here
Are bored silly, wouldn't you say?
Ain't nothing much for them to do,
'Cept getting drunk and cruising Main.
City kids have it made, don't they?
Get to see the latest movies,
Go to interesting places and all.
Nothing exciting happens around here,
Especially in winter, nothing at all.
Vern and I may go up to the Falls
And catch the basketball finals.
That might be exciting, don't you think?

Sylvia Cohen, Jason's Grandmother

When my son, Jason's father,
Started Little League,
I was there for every game,
Even though he sat on the bench most times.
When my daughter, Jason's aunt,
Started ballet lessons,
I went to every recital,
Even though she pirouetted in the back row of dancers.
When my granddaughter, Jason's sister,
Started art lessons at the museum on Saturdays,
I drove her there every week,
Even though her paintings did not win prizes.
I should do any less for my grandson?
I must confess basketball is a silly game to me,
Boys running up the court, down the court,
Up the court, down the court—always running.
But I will sit here and applaud for my grandson,
If he gets into the game, and even if he doesn't.
It is easy to cheer for the star
Who will light up the night.
It is more important to cheer for the star
Who doesn't shine as bright.

Nestor Padilla

Sweet Jesus,
I doubt you ever played basketball,
Releasing soft jumpers against
The backboard of heaven.
I doubt you ever brought the ball upcourt
Through a squad of seraphim toward
The backboard of heaven.
I doubt you ever wrestled a rebound
Away from Michael, the archangel, near
The backboard of heaven.
I don't mean to be disrespectful;
I don't mean to be rude.
But how can you possibly understand
What I am feeling right now
As I shake hands with the opposing players?
Let me have a good game tonight and
I promise I'll play ball with you
All the days of my life.
Please be on my side of the court,
Sweet Jesus, please.

Tamba Senesie

I had a house in Africa.
When most people hear my British accent,
And learn I am from the sub-Sahara,
They ask, trying to tease me,
"Are you Tarzan? Where is Jane?"
When most people hear I was born
In a small town outside of Lagos,
They ask, trying to be humorous,
"Are you the Lion King?"
When most people hear that my mother prepared meals
For a large extended family in our compound,
They ask, trying not to laugh out loud,
"Did she cook your relatives?"
Do I denigrate their culture?
Do I call all Americans barbarians?
As the African proverb goes:
"What the child says, he has heard at home."
Are the homes in America so
Overgrown by the tangled garden of ignorance,
Bare of the rich furniture of knowledge,
Open to the cold wind of cruelty?
I had a house in Africa.

Garrett James

I've played in tournaments 'round the country.
I've gone coast-to-coast,
From one baseline to another,
From one ocean to another.
I've flown over more time zones
Than I can remember.
But there is only one zone that counts,
Not the parking zone,
>   hospital zone,
>   loading zone,
>   commercial zone,
Not the combat zone,
>   red zone,
>   end zone,
>   neutral zone.
When I am in *THE ZONE*,
Every pass connects; every shot clicks.
I can't hear the crowd or the coach.
I am alone, alive, above the rim, above the arena,
Playin' in a zone for which there is no defense.
Nobody can ever hurt me up there.
I am untouchable.

 Tyrone Porter

When I told my little brother, who's ten,
I couldn't play ball because of heart problems,
He took it worse than me,
Throwin' hisself down on the ground and cryin'.
I wish I coulda done the same.
"You need a transplant or somethin'?"
He said between sobs.
"Yo, take mine,
I ain't no ballplayer, you is."
That broke me up.
But today I got better news for him:
The doc said I could play.
You bet I'm happy.
Look, you gotta excuse me,
I gotta call my little bro
And tell him I'm playin'.
He's gonna sit right behind me on the bench,
Wearin' his Tigers hat and my practice jersey,
Only a heartbeat away.

Roman Kirenova

My family had to flee Kiev
In middle of night.
There was not enough time to pack
More than single suitcase for each of us.
When I asked my father why, he said,
"There is no time to explain, just hurry."
"But what of my education?" I asked selfishly.
"You will learn while we travel," he replied.
Indeed.
I learned German in Vienna.
I learned Italian in Naples.
I learned French in Marseilles.
I am happy to report that
I can curse fluently in three languages.
Here, in America, I have unpacked my suitcase
For last time, I hope.
I go to school; I play ball.
Here, in America, I got called
For traveling in practice
And it had nothing to do with
Border patrols and customs offices.
I feel safe and secure here.
But my father
Keeps a bag packed by door,
Just in case.

Vonessa Leighton, Team Manager

"Roman, Roman, he's my man.
If he can't do it, no one can."
Me, tryin' out for cheerleading?
Yeah, right.
Roman, Roman, he's my man.
He's big, tall, and handsome.
He's white.
I'm small, short, and cute.
I'm black.
Together we'd make a delicious Black Russian.
Wouldn't that be a kick?
He's the one I want.
He's the one I gotta have.
Right before the game
Might be a bad time
To tell him he's mine, all mine.
But right after the game
I'm gonna hand check him so close
He'll think I'm inside his shirt.
Well? Not a bad place to be.
I will stick to him so tight,
He will see nothin' in front of him,
'Cept my smiley and sweaty face.
But even with me matchin' him step for step,
He's gonna have every chance to score.

Pete Nash, Bartender, The Inn
Joe Fromer, Town Resident

"You hear about the accident, Joe?"

"No."

"You didn't see all the ambulances?"

"No."

"You didn't hear the firehouse bells?"

"No."

"You didn't see all those state troopers?"

"No."

"Guess there's gonna be plenty of outsiders."

"Yeah."

"Maybe good for business, you think?"

"Yeah."

"Town's dead, ya know."

"Yeah."

"You want another beer, Joe?"

"Yeah."

Steven Walker

I work weekends in the real world,
In a pharmacy where I save my wages for college tuition.
My teammates live in the Land of Oz,
Where Nike endorsements and Wheaties promotions
Lie somewhere out of reach, just over the rainbow.
They all secretly hope
To play in the NBA, in the Emerald Cities of
Charlotte, Miami, Phoenix, or Portland.
They're all gonna be recruited by scouts.
They're all gonna get huge scholarships.
They're all gonna be picked by Division I schools.
They're all gonna turn pro.
They're all goin' nowhere,
All except James, who is the only one
With a ruby slipper for the Yellow Brick Road.
Me? I'll be thrilled if some Division III school calls.
Anyway, I got my plans figured out—
Goin' to study pharmacy
And one day have my own place.
As for my teammates, they can choose to travel
Down any dream road they want.
I only hope they don't choke
On the bitter pill of reality.

Z. Pratt

Lookie, lookie, at what I seen today
While helpin' my moms with her shoppin'.
It was my man, Walker, with his fan-cee
New job down at the CVS phar-ma-cee.
Who does the brother think he is?
Must be some upwardly mo-bile, light-skinned dude,
Workin' his way up a white ladder
With those lab-coated geeks
Who get a charge outta sayin' stuff like,
"Your prescription will be ready in an hour."
Hey, bro, get back to the 'hood.
You ain't no better than us,
Even if you tryin' to be.
Hey, bro, get back to your homeboys.
You ain't no different than us,
Even if you tryin' to be.
When you see that your new white friends
Will only work with you,
Not hang out with you,
You'll be back on the corner,
Or on the bench with us,
Chillin' and shootin' hoops.
I seen it all before.

Dennis Carleton

When I made the basketball team,
My father bought drinks
For all the guys down at the garage.
"When he was five I put up a hoop,"
He begins for the hundredth time,
"And practiced with my boy
All summer and nearly all winter."
I am the cup in his mental trophy case.
I am the plaque that hangs on his shop wall.
My permanent seat on the bench
Has not changed my father's dream one bit.
"You could score the game-winning jumper,
Or make the game-saving block," he says brightly.
"Dad, I'm a role player," I say, trying to explain,
"My job is to take a foul,
Or spell a starter for a minute or two."
"Don't talk like that," he says,
"You didn't think you'd make the team, I did."
My father still dreams,
Of buzzer-beaters and bragging rights,
And, of course, stories
He can tell the guys down at the garage.

Niki Carmichael, School Broadcaster

WELCOME, LADIES AND GENTLEMEN, TO TONIGHT'S
GAME. I'M NIKI CARMICHAEL, BRINGING YOU THE
FIRST GAME OF THE SEASON. THE STANDS ARE
PACKED, AND YOU CAN FEEL THE EXCITEMENT. THE
TEAMS ARE JUST FINISHING THEIR PRE-GAME WARM-
UPS, AND NOW, THE MOMENT WE'VE ALL BEEN
WAITING FOR. HERE IS THE STARTING LINEUP FOR
YOUR TOWER TIGERS: AT FORWARD, A SIX-FOOT-
THREE JUNIOR, NUMBER TWENTY-ONE, TYSHEEN
STANTON. AT THE OTHER FORWARD SPOT, A SIX-FOOT-
FOUR SENIOR, NUMBER TWENTY-THREE, DARNELL
JOYCE. AT THE CENTER SPOT, A SIX-FOOT-EIGHT
SENIOR, NUMBER THIRTY-TWO, TAMBA SENESIE.
AT THE GUARD POSITIONS, FIRST, A FIVE-FOOT-TEN
SOPHOMORE, NUMBER FOUR, NESTOR PADILLA. AND
LAST, BUT CERTAINLY NOT LEAST, *YOUR* ALL-CITY
GUARD, A SIX-FOOT-ONE SENIOR, NUMBER THIRTEEN,
GARRETT JAMES! THE COACH IS GREG HOSKINS. NOW
LET'S HEAR IT FOR THE TEAM. THANK YOU, LADIES
AND GENTLEMEN. WOULD YOU PLEASE RISE FOR OUR
NATIONAL ANTHEM . . .

Greg Hoskins, Coach

Hey, ref, they're killin' us out there.
> You missed that call, big time.
> Call it the same for both sides, zebra.
> Let one go against them for a change.
> You workin' for Eisenhower High?

Offense	**Defense**
Work, work, come on, Nestor,	Get your head into the game,
Good shot, Garrett,	Watch your man, Darnell,
Go up strong, Tamba,	Help in the middle, help,
Run 1W,	Who's got number twelve?
Tysheen, you got the shot, take it,	Trap, trap,
He's open for the three,	Play him tight, he's too open,
Good put-back, Tysheen,	Box him out, Darnell,
Reverse the ball,	No foul, no foul,
Nice play, guys.	Worst play I've seen.

Hey ref, watch the handchecking.
> He walked, too many steps.
> He got all ball, not his hand.
> Three seconds violation? Are you for real?
> You workin' for them?

You're calling a tech on me?
I didn't say a word, pal.

Basketball Pulse

```
                                              OOP
                                              —
                                    Y         S
       Bounce                       E         L
                    Bounce              L     A
Bounce                                 L      M
                          A                   D
       Bounce       Bounce                    U
                                              N
    Bounce       Bounce                       K
```

	D	D
	E	E
	F	F
	E	E
	N	N
	S	S
O	E	E

"MAN, DON'T EVEN THINK 'BOUT GETTIN' BY ME!"

Sharon Olivetti, CBS Anchor

THIS IS THE CBS EVENING NEWS. I'M SHARON OLIVETTI SITTING IN FOR DAN RATHER.

WE LEAD OFF TONIGHT WITH THE BLIZZARD OF THE DECADE. ACROSS THE EASTERN SEABOARD LIFE AND COMMERCE HAVE DRAMATICALLY HALTED. SNOW, LOTS OF IT, HAS BLANKETED THE NORTHEAST. MOTORISTS HAVE BEEN STRANDED, HOSPITALS HAVE BECOME SHELTERS, AND ALL AIRPORTS ARE SHUT DOWN.

IN WASHINGTON, D.C., GOVERNMENT OFFICES HAVE BEEN CLOSED FOR TWO DAYS. IN PROVIDENCE, RHODE ISLAND, STUDENTS FROM BROWN UNIVERSITY HAVE TRUDGED THROUGH HUGE SNOWDRIFTS TO BRING HOT MEALS TO PEOPLE TRAPPED IN THEIR HOUSES.

AND IN UPSTATE NEW YORK, NORTH OF ALBANY, WE HAVE REPORTS OF A TRAGIC BUS ACCIDENT. WE GO NOW TO OUR REPORTER, JUDY BENARES, FROM OUR AFFILIATE STATION WRGB IN ALBANY.

Dennis Carleton

Strained my arm,
Bit my tongue,
Wrenched my neck,
Hurt my lung.
Split my lip,
Scratched my eye,
Banged my head,
Bruised my thigh.
Crushed my nail,
Raised a cyst,
Turned my knee,
Sprained my wrist.
Pulled my leg,
Cut my gum,
Jabbed my hand,
Jammed my thumb.
Doctor, doctor,
Make a notation,
Get me into the
Starting rotation.

onessa Leighton, Team Manager

Roman, here's the way I picture it:
You're still keyed up from the game.
Of course you guys won.
Roman, you come off the bench,
Score in double figures,
And collect twelve boards.
You smell fresh from your shower.
Roman, you take me to a diner,
We sit and talk for hours.
Our hamburgers get cold
While you tell me every move you made.
Roman, you drive me home.
You kiss me passionately at my door.
Your hands start to move up my sides.
I tell you to stop, but I'm lyin'.

Roman Kirenova

"Vonessa, you see my sweats?
Catch you later, girl.
Guys, we going to diner
After game?"

Bernie Colchin, Local Businessman

You see, I'm usually sitting
At the register in my appliance store,
Watching a woman waddle across my hardwood floor,
Trying to decide which refrigerator she wants.
But now I'm sitting in the stands,
Cheering the present and remembering the past.
My mind darts back twenty years,
When I played guard on the hardwood floor at Tower
And scooped up more loose balls than anybody.
I had the floor burns to prove it.
We had a good team,
Made it to the quarterfinals
Of the city championships.
I could move then.
After watching Tower's first half,
I feel like going out
And shooting a few baskets.
I'm sure I'd throw up nothing but bricks.
I don't even have the energy to get up and stretch.

Frank DePrado, School Maintenance

As the clock winds down, I'm thinking,
If Garrett James were a doctor,
He'd be a surgeon, knifing through
Tissue-thin defenses.
If he were a lawyer,
He'd be a prosecutor whose slashing attacks
Would blow away the defense team.
If he were a priest,
He'd be an archbishop of the rim above
And convert all to the religion of basketball.
But he's only a kid,
And yet we lay our hopes and dreams
Across his athletic shoulders.
We pump the air with excitement
When he rises, gracefully,
Like some mythological bird and
Without a single wasted motion,
Lets fly a long, soft, sweet floater
That reminds us of what
Our lives could have been
Had time, dreams, and jump shots
Been frozen in a single Kodak moment
At age seventeen.

Greg Hoskins, Coach

Nestor, push the ball up!

Pick up, pick up number six

Garrett, look for your shot.

Switch, switch

Tysheen, fill the lane.

Some help, help, weak side

Tamba, post up.

Get up on your man

Tyrone, screen, screen.

Why'd you lose your man like that?

Time,
Time out!
What are you guys doin' out there?
Get your heads into the game, for God's sake.
Those guys came to play.
You guys came for a picnic.
Listen up, here's what we gotta do now.
Run 11B, and Garrett, you curl in behind
The screen and . . .
Porter, Porter, get up,
Stop foolin' around,
Porter!

Niki Carmichael, School Broadcaster

TIME HAS BEEN CALLED AT 5:43 OF THE THIRD
QUARTER, WITH THE TIGERS HOLDING A FOUR-POINT
LEAD, 47–43. THE EISENHOWER EAGLES HAVE BEEN
HANGING TOUGH. EXPECTATIONS WERE THAT THIS
WOULD BE A TIGER BLOWOUT, BUT THE EAGLES'
PRESSING DEFENSE AND THEIR ATTEMPTS TO DOUBLE-
TEAM JAMES HAVE SLOWED DOWN THE TIGER
OFFENSE. JAMES HAS SCORED A QUIET NINE POINTS,
BUT LOOK FOR HIM TO EXPLODE AT CRUNCH TIME.
HE HAS WOWED THE CROWD THUS FAR, WITH HIS
SPECTACULAR PASSING, ONCE TO A CUTTING PADILLA,
WHO PUT IT IN FOR AN EASY DEUCE, AND ONCE TO A
WIDE-OPEN STANTON, WHO BURIED THE TEN-FOOT
JUMPER. SENESIE HAS BEEN STRONG OFF THE BOARDS.
PORTER HAS JUST COME IN FOR JOYCE, UP FRONT.
THE HORN HAS SOUNDED, AND I LOOK FOR JAMES TO—
WAIT A SECOND, THERE'S A PLAYER DOWN ON THE
COURT, NEAR THE TIGER BENCH. I CAN'T SEE WHO IT IS.

Sharif Daniels, Student Fan

Hey, you see that?

Who went down?

I can't see who it is from here.

I bet it was a fight.

One of their guys must've

Come over and thrown a punch.

They must still have it in for us.

Remember last year when the ref

Called their guy for steps

Right before he threw in the tyin' basket?

One guy punched out the ref,

But he wasn't even arrested.

You see who it is yet?

Hope it ain't James.

If he's hurt we can kiss the season good-bye.

Porter?

Porter who?

Hey, man, he's only a sub.

He don't matter.

Just drag him outta there already

And get this game started again.

What's holdin' things up?

n Patrol

This is Unit Five.
Yeah, got it.
On our way.
Some disturbance up at the high school.
Hope no one got killed.
Remember that history teacher from a few years ago?
Yeah, Tower High, they didn't say.
No, I don't know where the school cop is.
Either at the game or in the lounge, I bet.
I could deal with that kind of shift.
So what's your guess?
Trouble at the game?
Team's different this year, I hear.
Got this kid
Who's supposed to be the real deal.
Yeah, big-time colleges
Are after him, in his shorts, I hear.
Hope this don't take long,
I'm hungry.
You want Italian or Chinese?
I don't care.
You know, I went to that school.
Sure hasn't changed much.
Ain't nobody ever made the pros from there.

THIRD QUARTER: BOX SCORE SUMMARIES

5, 4, 3, 2, 1—Cue Tim

THIS IS TIM McHALE REPORTING FOR SPORTSCABLE 3. TONIGHT WE CONTINUE OUR SERIES ON THE SURGING TIGERS OF TOWER HIGH. SO FAR, THERE IS NOTHING TO SUGGEST THAT PRESEASON EXPECTATIONS WERE WRONG. IN THEIR FIRST FOUR GAMES THE TIGERS HAVE CHEWED, MAULED, AND BATTERED THEIR OPPONENTS BY AN AVERAGE OF TWENTY-TWO POINTS. LED BY GARRETT JAMES, WHO IS AVERAGING TWENTY-SIX POINTS PER GAME, THE TIGERS' BIGGEST CHALLENGE SEEMS TO BE COMPLACENCY. THE TIGERS ARE SO TOP-HEAVY WITH TALENT, FEW, IF ANY TEAMS, CAN MATCH UP WITH THEM. GARRETT JAMES, THE SENSATIONAL SENIOR GUARD, IS NOT THE WHOLE STORY: SENESIE IS A TOWER OF STRENGTH UNDER THE BOARDS. PADILLA COMPLEMENTS JAMES IN THE BACKCOURT. AND UP FRONT, STANTON HAS FOUND THE RANGE WITH HIS JUMPER, WHILE JOYCE IS STELLAR ON DEFENSE. THIS IS A SOLID, WELL-COACHED SQUAD. ONE UNHAPPY NOTE: TYRONE PORTER, THE PROMISING JUNIOR, IS STILL IN SERIOUS BUT STABLE CONDITION FOLLOWING HIS COLLAPSE IN

THE TIGERS' HOME OPENER. WE WISH HIM A SPEEDY
RECOVERY, AND WE HOPE THE TEAM ENJOYS
CONTINUED SUCCESS.

Tower Tigers Cheer

Tiger, tiger, burning bright,
Tiger power, Tiger might.
Pawed 'em,
Sawed 'em,
Ate 'em,
Gnawed 'em.
Tiger, tiger, burning bright,
Tiger power, Tiger might.
Trapped 'em,
Zapped 'em,
Floored 'em,
Rapped 'em.
Our immortal hand or eye,
We're Tiger power, hear our cry.
Tiger, tiger, burning bright,
Tiger power, Tiger might.

Sharif Daniels

The other kid's OK?
That's good,
I don't like to see nobody get hurt.
You came to see my man, James, play?
Ain't he somethin', though?
You play him up close,
He's past you on the first dribble.
Lay off of 'im,
And he nails you with the three.
And his defense—
You wanna talk about his defense?
He wraps up his man so tight,
The dude thinks he is inside a cocoon.
Selfish?
My man ain't selfish.
You see the way he dishes off.
My own life?
You wanna talk about my life?
It ain't nothin', man.
The only time I come close
To being alive is when
I see my man, James, play.
Hope he stays healthy a good, long time.
Wouldn't want nothin' bad happenin' to him.

Garrett James

After a game,
They throw themselves at me,
Like sharply angled passes.
They shadow my every move,
Like quick-steppin' guards.
They listen to my every word,
Like I was a senator or somethin'.
After a game,
After my shower,
They hang around the door of the locker room,
Waitin' to trap me,
Waitin' to invite me
To this one's party
Or that one's house
For a little one-on-one contact.
Don't get me wrong:
I love the ladies.
I love to put the moves on them,
Nothin' serious, just a little flirtin'.
But I would like it even better
If they would wait for me in the stands
Until I decided who I wanted to talk with,
Instead of attackin' me
With their full-court press.

Noelle Williams

Hush, little baby, my little one,
Papa's gonna make you a Phoenix Sun.
If that Phoenix Sun gets beat,
Papa's gonna make you a Miami Heat.
If that Miami Heat don't fold,
Papa's gonna keep you from the cold.
If the weather ain't too chilly,
Papa's gonna send you north to Philly.
If you aren't happy there, my pet,
Papa's gonna make you a Jersey Net.
If that Jersey net's too fine,
Papa's gonna shoot from beyond the line.
If from that line he hits the J,
You know for sure he's made the NBA.
If he works and has some luck,
Papa might become a Milwaukee Buck.
Hush, little baby, don't cry at all,
Papa's gonna buy you a basketball.
And if that ball ain't got no name,
Your papa's gonna sign it "Garrett James."

Noelle Williams

Some people say I got pregnant
To trap Garrett into a relationship.
Some people say I had the baby
To tap into the millions Garrett's sure to get.
Some people are full of shit.
I didn't mean for it to happen,
But what do you want me to do—
Give up this precious package,
Mark him as junk male,
And stamp across his little forehead,
RETURN TO SENDER?
Some people say, "You lucky, girl,
You win the grand prize.
The check is on its way."
Hey, my baby ain't no door prize
In the Garrett James Sweepstakes.
He ain't guaranteed no free,
All-expense-paid trip to
The Promised Land of the NBA.
I love my little boy,
My Special Delivery little boy,
Whether or not his father makes it big.

E. Z. Pratt

When I came to this school,
You said you would take care of me.
You said not to worry 'bout nothin'
'Cept playin' basketball.
You promised me tutors.
You promised me easy teachers
Who, with a wink and a smile,
Would let me slide.
Then, all of a sudden,
You changed the rules on me.
You expected me to go to class,
Do work, pass tests.
So, now, when I've failed my classes
You tell me I can't play no more.
How come you're jerkin' me around?
You wouldn't do that
If I was Garrett James.
You lied.
You didn't let me sink baskets.
You just let me sink.
Man, you sure took care of me.

Tamba Senesie

When the bus driver said one day,
"Get to the back of the bus,"
I thought he was just providing
More room for us.
When the bus driver said the next day,
"I bet you are a good basketball player,"
I thought he was just complimenting me
On my strong and straight body.
When the bus driver said the following day,
"Just look at those fine black boys,"
I thought he was just trying to
Engage me in some friendly conversation.
When my teammate, Tysheen, informed me
That our bus driver was extremely racist,
I was very much shocked indeed.
In America, it's quite difficult to understand
That what people say with their mouths
Reflects not what they mean with their hearts.

Judy Benares, WRGB Reporter

THIS IS JUDY BENARES, REPORTING TO YOU LIVE FROM JUST OUTSIDE THE PICTURESQUE TOWN OF HUDSON LANDING, NESTLED IN THE FOOTHILLS OF THE ADIRONDACKS, WHERE TODAY A SCHOOL BUS CARRYING A HIGH SCHOOL BASKETBALL TEAM TO THE STATE FINALS AT GLENS FALLS CRASHED THROUGH A GUARDRAIL AND TUMBLED DOWN AN EMBANKMENT. LOCAL AMBULANCES RESPONDED QUICKLY AND TOOK THE INJURED TO GLENS FALLS MEMORIAL, AS WELL AS OTHER AREA HOSPITALS. AT THIS POINT WE DO NOT HAVE AN EXACT COUNT OF THE DEAD AND INJURED, BUT ACCORDING TO STATE TROOPER KEVIN MORAN, ONE OF THE FIRST OFFICERS ON THE SCENE, "THE CASUALTIES HAVE BEEN CONSIDERABLE." TROOPER MORAN, WHAT CAN YOU TELL US?

Nestor Padilla

When I go back to visit Puerto Rico,
All my relatives say with enthusiasm,
"Here comes the Yankee basketball boy.
He will win a big scholarship
And go to the finest university."
When I come back to America,
My mother says with sarcasm,
"Here comes the jalapeño basketball boy.
He will win a big scholarship
And go to the finest university."
She says this after seeing my report card,
Which barely has a passing average.
"For basketball you have time, *muchacho,*
Not for studying?"
I say to her, "It's your fault, Mama.
In Puerto Rico I was smart; here I am dumb.
It's because you mix me up in two languages."
"Dumb is dumb in any language," she answers.
It's why I like basketball—no language, just math.
It's as easy as:
Uno—foul shot,
Dos—field goal,
Tres—three-point bomb.

Darnell Joyce

It's like I'm playin' with four personal fouls.
One more and I'm outta there.
Coach says my head ain't in the game,
And he ain't talkin' about just basketball.
I don't eat right.
I don't sleep right.
I don't study right.
I stay out late a lot,
Thinkin' about stuff in circles.
My teachers say my head ain't in the game, either,
And they ain't talkin' about just exams.
When my counselor, Ms. Chartoff,
Called me down to her office,
I couldn't tell her nothin'
'Cept to say I been throwin' up bricks lately.
If she didn't quite understand my words,
She did understand my feelings.
"Who takes care of you, big guy?" she asked.
"No one," I said, bitin' my lip.
I had to step outside her office.
I couldn't let her see me cry.

# Jason Cohen

Together we look like
Mutt and Jeff,
Abbott and Costello,
DeVito and Schwarzenegger.
When we go to the diner, his friends say,
"Yo, who's the little white boy you're hangin' with?"
He says, "He's my bro. You got a problem with that?"
He's been over to my house so many times,
My grandma wants to adopt him.
He stays at my house a lot.
His home life ain't too cool,
So we don't talk about it much.
He does my math homework; I do his history.
We sit at the kitchen table,
Studying our books and stuffing our faces.
"Hey, ugly," he says,
"Your grandma got more of that soup?"
"You mean the one with the noodles?"
"Yeah, that's what I want."
"Lots."
Friendship, I guess, is just a matter of taste.

Jason Cohen

I may not be a marquee player.
I may not be announced
In the opening credits of the starting lineup.
But you better believe,
In front of the lights and mikes,
I'm gonna make the most
Of my few minutes upon the hardwood stage.
You watch my acting as I take charge.
You watch my leaping as I pull down a rebound.
You watch my emoting as I trash-talk my man.
Let Garrett take star billing.
Let Tamba play a featured role.
I don't take offense, guys.
I'm happier on defense, anyway.
If I steal the ball, I've stolen the scene.
If I shut down my man, I've upstaged him.
I may not be a marquee player,
I'm more like a short subject.
But I hope my coach applauds
The intensity of my performance.

Vonessa Leighton

"A Poem for Roman" by Vonessa Leighton

Waiting for you, Roman,

Takes my time,

But I will wait for you

For all the seconds and minutes of the game.

Loving you, Roman,

Takes my time,

But I will wait for you

For all the weeks and months of the schedule.

Sorrow, too,

Takes my time,

But I will wait for you

'Til hell freezes over,

Or the end of the basketball season,

Whichever comes first.

Then, we will meet in the darkened arena,

Kiss under the basket,

And twirl in the embrace of

Courtly love.

Roman Kirenova

Give me wild Mongol thundering toward me.
Give me driving snow of Siberian winter.
Give me searing heat of Ukrainian summer.
Give me Gulag,
But keep that girl away from me.
I'd rather walk steppes barefoot.
I'd rather swim Volga naked.
I'd rather face siege of Stalingrad unarmed.
Give me Gulag,
But keep that girl away from me.
What does she want?
We are from two different levels.
I am foot and a half taller.
It would be most strange, I think,
If we walk down street together.
I try to tell her we can't see eye to eye,
But she will not take no for answer.
I wish only to shoot ball into net.
I do not wish to get trapped in hers.

Tyrone Porter

My mom blames the school.
The school blames the doctors.
The doctors blame my aunt.
She blames God,
For me being as stupid as I am.
I don't blame nobody.
It just is, that's all.
Ain't nothin' I can do 'bout it,
But play some ball and have a good time.
When they gave out smarts,
I wasn't in the startin' lineup.
When they taught me to read,
I wasn't even payin' attention.
I can just 'bout sign my name,
Which is OK for autographs and stuff.
No, I don't blame God at all,
But I think he coulda gave me
A head and a heart in better working condition,
Somethin' that comes with a lifetime guarantee.

Kevin Moran, State Trooper

That's right, I was the first on the scene,
A minute or two before the ambulances.
What did I see?
Well, let me put it to you this way, ma'am:
When I was a kid,
We used to have this game called
Pick-up sticks—you know what that is?
You toss these sticks out of your hands
And they fall on top of each other.
You have to pick them up one at a time
Without moving any of the others.
It was like these kids were the sticks,
Tossed out of God's hands, all in a jumble.
The people in the bus went flying.
Some got tossed through the windows;
Some just fell over each other, and
Some sticks just snapped.
I didn't know which stick to touch first.
I didn't know which broken one to pick up.
I was thankful when the ambulance arrived.

Nestor Padilla

The bounce of the ball,
The cadence of the crowd,
The pulse of the players,
I hear that salsa beat.
The *tiempo* of the timbales,
The bang of the bass,
The kick of the congas,
I hear that salsa beat.
I bring the ball up court,
The music pounding in my brain.
Garrett rifles the orange to me,
A straight, true line of melody.
I fake right, go left,
Matching the rhythm that's in my head.
I penetrate the lane, bodies all around,
One step, two steps, get out of my way.
Pivot, twist, back to the circle,
Kick, kick, kick it on out.
Garrett jumps, he hangs, he shoots.
Hands, hands, follow through.
Swish, swish, the sound of the street,
Basketball, basketball, move to the beat.

Tysheen Stanton

In my father's house,
I am the prisoner who gets parole
If I can successfully answer
A series of questions at the front door checkpoint.
"Where are you going?"
"What are you doing?"
"When will you be back?"
And after telling the necessary lies,
I am allowed a few hours of freedom
Before returning to the solitary confinement of my room.
In my father's house,
He raises the roof if I get out of line.
He bars the door to my friends.
He invades my space, my room, without knocking.
He undermines my foundation
By tearing me down brick by brick.
One day I'd like to leave my father's house,
Break the lease that binds us,
And live in my own place,
Unattached.

Greg Hoskins, Coach

You wanna know why
I called this extra practice?
You wanna know why
I am not a happy camper?
Tell me if this rings a bell or two:
Dropped passes,
Blown shots,
Lousy foul-shooting.
You want more?
No looking for the open man,
No hitting the offensive boards,
No helping out on defense.
All of you are walking around
With your mind on other things.
But you're gonna say, "We're winning, Coach."
I'm gonna say, "We're winning ugly."
And ugly teams do not dance at the play-off ball.
If we aren't careful,
A Cinderella team might slip in with the victory,
And, speaking for myself,
This coach has absolutely no desire
To turn into a smashed pumpkin.
All right, starters, step up, start moving.
It's your turn to get out on the floor.

Dennis Carleton

I walked into the gym,
After having missed practice the day before.
Coach looked at me, his eyes asking the question.
I looked down, not having the answer.
He just pointed to the bench,
As my teammates jogged through their warm-up laps.
In our next game I didn't play at all,
Not even in garbage time.
Afterward, in the quiet of the empty bleachers,
I slammed my hand against the scorer's table.
It was then I realized I was hurting
Not only myself, but my team as well.
In the silent argument between us,
It was Coach with no words to say
Who had spoken loudest of all.

Greg Hoskins, Coach

Four minutes to go?
We still got a shot.
I called this time-out
Because I want you to remember
What it feels like to be losing.
You guys have had it way too easy,
Been believing your press clippings.
But the only thing being written today
Is this game's obituary.
What are we, down by ten?
We still got a shot, if you give it a shot.
Tamba—you're letting your man get position on you.
Darnell—you're taking jumpers from Mars.
Nestor—you're losing your man on the switch.
Tysheen—you're allowing number eleven to drive right by you.
And Garrett—you're trying to do it all yourself.
This ain't Tiger basketball, this is playground ball.
And unless I see some heart out there,
There is gonna be some
Serious pine time for some of you.
OK, guys, let's get to work out there.
Look for the open man.
We still got a shot.

Basketball Pulse

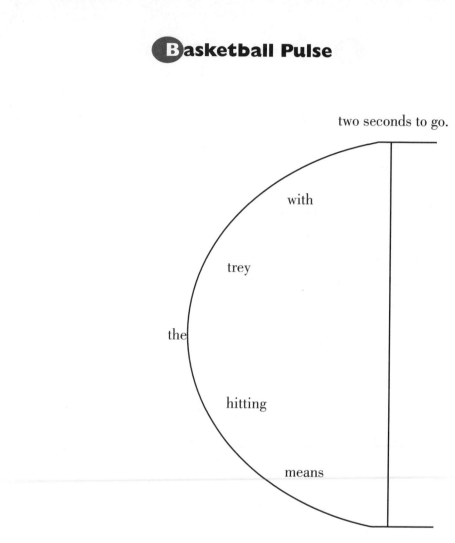

two seconds to go.

with

trey

the

hitting

means

Life of Circle The

Basketball Pulse

Rebound:

In
the
of

my

life,

game

Which
ball

is   the

way

going

to

bounce?

Mary Beth Hoskins

My husband has promised
Not to take the game home with him.
My husband is a liar.
My husband has promised
Not to spend all his waking hours in the gym.
My husband is a deceiver.
My husband has promised
Not to coach next year.
My husband is a prevaricator.
He is particularly bad after a loss.
If my in-laws want to speak to him,
They had better fill the passing lanes.
If my parents want to speak to him,
They had better schedule a conference.
If I want to speak to him,
I have to call, "Time-out!"
During the season, I have learned to lay up
With an armful of elegant romance novels
And dream of kings and queens
Dancing gracefully on courts of their own.
During the off-season, I can press Greg
For a few one-on-one practice sessions
And dream of expanding our own family team,
Knowing it's all the playing time I can get.

Debbie Caffrey, Ambulance Driver

You could hardly see
Outta the front window.
You could hardly hear
Over the wind's howl.
You could hardly drive
Over the ice-encrusted road.
But me and McGrory busted ass
To get up there, once we heard
It was a school bus that went off the road.
Got kids of my own, you know.
We were the first ambulance
To reach the scene.
I heard the screaming 'fore I saw
The bodies lying at odd angles
In and out of the bus.
Some were dead; some were dying.
We covered, injected, splinted,
Comforted, as best we could.
It wasn't enough.
There was too much blood
For McGrory and me.
We waited for backup.
Red blood on white snow
Turns pink, you know.

Niki Carmichael, School Broadcaster

GOOD MORNING, TOWER FAMILY. HERE ARE TODAY'S
HOMEROOM ANNOUNCEMENTS: THE DRAMA CLUB
WILL HOLD AUDITIONS AFTER SCHOOL TODAY IN
ROOM 311 FOR ITS MUSICAL VERSION OF *WAR AND
PEACE*. THE OUTDOORS CLUB WILL HOLD ITS FIRST
MEETING AFTER SCHOOL TODAY IN ROOM 104 ON
ACCOUNT OF THE RAIN. PRINCIPAL LEEKS REMINDS
EVERYONE THAT WINDOWS CANNOT BE OPENED MORE
THAN SIX INCHES FROM THE BOTTOM. AND FINALLY,
YOUR BASKETBALL BRAVEHEARTS, AFTER A TOUGH
LOSS TO THE AMBASSADORS OF CARTER HIGH, 71–65,
REBOUNDED WITH A CONVINCING WIN OVER WILSON,
78–52, FOLLOWED BY AN 80–47 THRASHING OF
McKINLEY. AND YESTERDAY, IN A CLOSE ONE, OUR
TIGERS CLAWED PAST FILLMORE HIGH, 67–64. THE
TIGERS SEEM TO BE ON A ROLL AND WILL NEXT MEET
THE WILDCATS OF GARFIELD HIGH NEXT TUESDAY.
ROAR, TIGERS, ROAR. THAT'S ALL THE NEWS FROM
THE TOP OF THE TOWER. THIS IS NIKI CARMICHAEL
REPORTING TO YOU LIVE.

Garrett James

I pick,
I roll,
I score
A goal.
I square,
I shoot,
I'm fouled
To boot.
I block,
I shake,
I run
The break.
I fake,
I move,
I'm in
The groove.
Word up,
'Nuff said,
No ball?
I'm dead.

Garrett James

Mr. Paley, my history teacher,
Ain't too impressed with me.
No matter how many points I get,
Steals I make, rebounds I grab,
My stats don't matter to him.
I start to argue; he begins,
"Mr. James, in the cosmic scope of events,
The world will little note, nor long remember,
Who won the high school championship
This year, last year, or any year."
I continue to argue; he goes on,
"Mr. James, in eons to come, future archaeologists
Will unearth a deflated basketball,
Think it some round animal, and will wonder
At the meaning of the brand NBA upon it."
I argue louder; he goes right on,
"Mr. James, become someone who can leave a legacy,
A teacher, perhaps, yes, you'd be a good one.
I see the younger students following you in the halls.
You have natural leadership abilities."
I thank him; he has one more thing to say,
"Mr. James, do something useful with your life.
That is the way you can score points with me."

Eldon Jackson, Garrett James's Cousin

The projects is like a vacuum cleaner, man.

Sucks you up, messes you up, and keeps you inside

Until you're ready to be disposed of.

Everyone has the same brand-name dreams about getting out—

Ads for Adidas, commercials for Converse—

But the vacuum cleaner sucks 'em all back.

You think I didn't have Garrett's dreams?

You think I didn't wanna play ball?

Man, ten years later I still have those dreams,

Only now they're in Garrett.

When he was little, I took him to the courts

And dribbled over, around, and through him.

Knocked him over so much, he learned to bounce back up,

Like one of those Weebles people.

Now he can blow right past me without blinking,

Rain threes on my head and knock me down.

I may be the one stuck in the vacuum cleaner,

With all the dirt and grime of this neighborhood,

But my boy, Garrett, my little Weebles cuz,

He's the one who's gonna clean up.

And when his time comes,

When he makes it to the top,

I'm gonna be right there,

Dressed in my cleanest, fanciest suit.

Rayanne Walker, Steven's Mother

I was fifteen when I had Raymond.
Didn't know any better then and thought
You couldn't get pregnant the first time.
Both father and son didn't amount to much.
I sees them in the neighborhood sometimes,
Doin' their dope shit with the other men on the corner.
I was twenty when I had Steven.
Amazin' how little I learned in five years,
Seein' how his father skipped, too.
Steven's father didn't amount to much, either.
I sees him in the neighborhood sometimes,
Doin' his car shit with the other men on the corner.
I was thirty-seven when I finally got my own shit together
And found me a regular job in the nursing home.
I get up each morning to go to work.
Steven gets up each morning to go to school.
I get up each Sunday morning to go to church.
Steven gets up each Sunday morning to go to church.
I go to school three nights a week to become a registered nurse.
Steven goes to work three nights a week to earn college money.
Next week is his birthday.
All I can say is God bless my darlin' boy.
I'm gonna cook him all his favorite things
And celebrate the fact that
We is one small, happy family.

Daisy Mejías

When my parents fight,
I run into my room, shut my eyes,
And wait for the noisy round to end.
Afterward,
My father retires to the TV in the living room,
My mother to the radio in the bedroom.
I catch my breath and wonder
What small incident or slight
Will ring the bell for their next fight.
I don't want a marriage like that, no way.
My boyfriend, Steven, and I have begun to talk,
Not about his basketball or my shopping,
Not about his job at the pharmacy
Or my job at the video store.
We talk softly about important stuff, like:
How beautiful the wedding's gonna be,
Where we want to live,
How many kids we want.
I figure the more talking we do now,
The less fighting we'll do later on.
The more we hold each other now,
The less we'll scrap later on.
I'm not saying marriage is a perfect mix,
But I'd like to keep the fights between us quiet
And not play them out in a public arena.

Steven Walker

Hey, Bill, closin' time yet?
My mama's fixin' some delicious food—
Beats that junk you're always eatin'.

Hey, man, we're closin' soon.
Don't you see my manager
Shuttin' off the lights?
Do I got what?
Hey, man, put that thing down.
Hey, man, be cool, don't fool with that.
Yeah, yeah, I'm openin' the register
As quick as I can.
No, I know you ain't foolin' around.
The drawer's stuck,
No, really.

Why'd you shoot me, man?
I was doin' what you said.
I wasn't causin' you any trouble.
Why'd you . . .
Mama,
Mama.

FOURTH QUARTER: PLAY-OFFS AND BEYOND

5. 4, 3, 2, 1—Cue Tim

THIS IS TIM McHALE, REPORTING FOR SPORTSCABLE 3. TONIGHT, WE RETURN TO THE TIGERS' GYM, WHERE TRAGEDY HAS STRUCK TOWER HIGH SCHOOL ONCE MORE. WHILE JUNIOR SWINGMAN TYRONE PORTER HAS FULLY RECOVERED FROM HIS COLLAPSE IN THE HOME OPENER, WE ARE SADDENED TO REPORT THAT STEVEN WALKER, A RESERVE GUARD, WAS SHOT AND KILLED DURING A ROBBERY AT A LOCAL PHARMACY LAST NIGHT. ACCORDING TO BILL LACY, THE STORE MANAGER, A LONE GUNMAN ENTERED THE STORE AT CLOSING TIME, WENT TO THE COUNTER, AND AFTER A FEW SECONDS, FIRED A SINGLE SHOT, THEN RAN OUT. POLICE ARE ASKING ANYONE WITH INFORMATION TO CONTACT THE LOCAL PRECINCT AT THE NUMBER BELOW. MEANWHILE, FAMILY AND TEAMMATES ARE DEVASTATED. WE TRIED TO CATCH UP WITH COACH GREG HOSKINS, BUT HE, AS WELL AS THE TEAM, WAS TOO DISTRAUGHT TO SPEAK TO US ON CAMERA. WHAT THIS WILL DO TO THE FORTUNES OF THE TIGER TEAM, WHO ARE HEAVILY FAVORED IN THE PLAY-OFFS AND BEYOND, IS ANYBODY'S GUESS. FUNERAL ARRANGEMENTS HAVE NOT YET BEEN ANNOUNCED.

FROM ALL OF US HERE AT SPORTSCABLE 3, OUR CONDOLENCES GO OUT TO MRS. WALKER AND HER FAMILY, AS WELL AS TO THE WHOLE TOWER HIGH SCHOOL COMMUNITY.

Tower Tigers Cheer

Tiger, tiger, burning bright,
Jump right into the spotlight.
Tiger b-ball,
Tiger bounce,
Watch us battle,
Watch us pounce.
Tiger, tiger, burning bright,
Jump right into the spotlight.
Tiger quickness,
Tiger bite,
Tigers, Tigers,
Feast tonight.
Yes, immortal hand or eye,
We will win, you can't deny.
Tiger, tiger, burning bright,
Jump right into the spotlight.

Rayanne Walker, Steven's Mother

"Praised Be the Lord"

They'll wear his number eighteen on their jerseys.
They'll bring flowers to the spot he died.
They'll offer a scholarship in his name.
They'll hang a plaque on the wall.

"Oh Happy Day"

The minister will say the right words.
The principal will say the kind words.
The coach will say the healing words.
The newspaper will say the wrong words.

"His Is the Power"

It don't matter that it all makes no sense.
It don't matter that my life is shattered.
It don't matter that he was a good boy.
It don't matter that they may catch his killer.

"He Shall Reign on Earth"

God or Man,
Heaven or Earth,
This is what matters:
How could you have allowed this to happen?
How could you have taken my baby,
My darling little baby boy?

"Amen"

Reverend Clayton Osborne Jr.

He's with the Lord's team now.
Brother Steven is with the Lord's team now.
Say amen, say amen, hallelujah!
He's dribbling with the angels for all eternity.
He's showering the ether with rainbow floaters.
He's grabbing the rebounds off the rim of Heaven.
And he's shooting like a comet
Across the canopy of stars.
There is no pain up there,
Only happiness and winning baskets.
There is no fear up there,
Only harmony and good passes.
There is no loneliness up there,
Only fellowship and perimeter shooting.
Steven will never play on a losing side
With God as his celestial coach
And the seraphim keeping score.
Steven will rejoice on Heaven's playground,
Everlasting.
Say amen, brothers and sisters,
Say amen, now.

Patrick Whitley, Reporter

I know this is a difficult moment for you, Coach,
But I wonder if you would tell me about,
Let me see my notes, yes, Shaun Walker,
Excuse me, Steven Walker.
His death had to do with drugs, did it not?
Oh, he worked in a pharmacy.
Excuse me, I was given a different story.
Basketball was his whole life, wasn't it?
Oh, he wanted to be a pharmacist.
Excuse me, I was told the wrong information.
What kind of music did he like, rap, no?
You don't say, classical music, really?
Oh, I didn't think they enjoyed that.
Excuse me, I meant no offense.
What do you mean,
"There is no excuse" for me?

Tamba Senesie

I hope no one objects that
I have called this players' meeting
To address a serious problem.
No doubt we will achieve the play-offs,
But we lack a moral purpose
To guide us in our athletic quest.
Might it not be too presumptuous to suggest
That we dedicate our season
To our fallen teammate, Steven Walker?
I have been in America but a short time
And have seen with my own eyes
How quickly people are prone to point out
What separates rather than what unites them.
For Steven's sake, can we not put to rest
Old scars, old hurts, old injustices
And join together in the spirit of
Brotherhood and fair play?
Working together,
We can build a team,
Or a nation.

Roman Kirenova

Check, Boris,
You are not concentrating on game.
Do you not see your king is trapped?
What do you mean, I'm the one who is trapped?
You are wrong, my friend,
I do not think of her at all.
I do not see her face
When I practice my foul shots.
I do not see her face
When I run my twenty laps.
I do not see her face
When she hands me water bottle.
This Russian and that American
Are poles apart, really we are.
Stop grinning, you're in check again.
What do you mean, I am one to be checkmated?
Do you not see how much room I have to maneuver?
Stop laughing, she will never capture me.
Even though there is no holding her in check.

Victor Tuttle, College Coach

I know a lot of colleges want you, Garrett,
But you should make ours your first choice.
Let me tell you why:
First and foremost, we're family.
We do everything together:
We eat together;
We win together;
We celebrate together.
You're looking for serious playing time?
I can guarantee you'll start.
You're looking for social activities?
I can guarantee you parties every night.
You're looking for academics?
I can guarantee we got 'em.
(I can get you some information on that later.)
Come to our beautiful campus and
Your name will be on everybody's lips.
You'll be on TV and in tournaments.
You'll have the attention of the best
Group of assistant coaches in the land.
You'll also have my personal attention.
Anything you want, we can get for you.
Excuse me, though, what time is it?
I do have another appointment, you understand.
Don't worry, you are my odds-on first choice.
I can guarantee you that.

Albert Goodson, Church Elder

What makes a bus slip to the right?
    A twist of the road,
    A twist of the wheel,
    A twist of fate.
What makes a bus veer off the road?
    A turn to the right,
    A turn to the left,
    A turn toward oblivion.
What makes a bus jump the guardrail?
    A matter of capriciousness,
    A matter of karma,
    A matter of kismet.
What makes a bus roll over and over?
    A question of indecision,
    A question of incompetence,
    A question of indifference—
    The cosmic kind.
Lord have mercy.
May the children heal
So that their mothers
Never have to sing
A dirge for the dead.

arrett James

When I was six,
Before my father split,
He used to take me to the old merry-go-round,
The worn-out one that stood
At the edge of the park,
Like some homeless person.
I'd sit on the cracked horses
And dream of real ones,
As I heard my father yell,
"Reach for the ring, Garrett,
Reach for the ring."
Everyone tells me,
Go to this college or that basketball camp,
Like they all want to catch the reins of my life
And lead me in the direction
They want me to go.
Maybe I want to ride down my own trail,
Follow my own path and shoot for the pros,
Right now.
The hell with going around in circles.
I ain't a kid anymore.
I hear the old merry-go-round finally broke down.
I also hear my father's back in the neighborhood.
Wonder what he wants.

Niki Carmichael, School Broadcaster

GOOD MORNING, TOWER FAMILY, HOW ARE WE DOING? HERE ARE TODAY'S HOMEROOM ANNOUNCEMENTS: PRINCIPAL LEEKS HAS ANNOUNCED THERE WILL BE A MEMORIAL SERVICE FOR STEVEN WALKER TO BE HELD FRIDAY, IN THE SCHOOL AUDITORIUM AT 2 P.M. THE DEBATE TEAM WILL COMPETE THIS AFTERNOON AGAINST POLK HIGH SCHOOL IN ROOM 227 AFTER EIGHTH PERIOD. THE TOPIC IS: SHOULD HANDGUNS BE OUTLAWED? THE MUSIC CLUB REMINDS PEOPLE TO ATTEND THE SPRING CONCERT. TICKETS ARE AVAILABLE IN ROOM 147. AND FINALLY, IN BASKETBALL THIS WEEK, DESPITE THE RECENT TRAGEDY, THE VARSITY DEFEATED GARFIELD, 82–75, AND BUCHANAN, 79–73, TO CLINCH A PLAY-OFF SPOT. ROAR, TIGERS, ROAR. HAVE A GOOD DAY, TOWER.

Tysheen Stanton

My father doesn't talk to me.
He has worries of his own.
The company he works for
May go out of business soon.
He is too young to retire,
And too old to start over.
Late at night, when I go to the fridge
To grab a glass of milk,
I see him at the kitchen table,
Deciding which bills to pay
And which ones to postpone.
He looks up at me as I pass by
But doesn't say a word.
Putting the milk back,
I see a note held in place
By a small refrigerator magnet
That looks like a little basketball.
It is an announcement from the local paper
Of the day and time of our first play-off game.
I go quietly back to my room,
Being careful not to disturb my father,
Who is still busy with paper and pencil.
My father speaks to me,
Some.

Valdeen DeForest

We were in the fight of our lives.
We battled on our hands and knees,
Knowing if anyone dropped the ball,
We would face certain defeat.
We repelled their attacks.
We took their best shots,
Knowing if we didn't meet their challenge,
We would face certain destruction.
Had it been a street fight,
There would be casualties all around.
Had it been a pitched battle,
There would be a body count.
I jumped, loaded up,
And struck down with such force,
My shot totally decimated the enemy,
Their bodies littering the ground.
A fight, a battle, a war?
Yeah, all that.
We just won the girls' city volleyball championship.
Did you read about it in the papers?
Any mention of it at all?
Just basketball news—the coming play-offs.
Right.

Greg Hoskins, Coach

Publicity is a poison,
Like a cup of wine
That can raise a man to drunken heights
Only to crash him down into frightening depths.
It works on his mind,
Making him think he's better than he is.
And you guys have been sipping at that cup,
Getting high on clippings and interviews.
Publicity makes a person sail in polluted waters,
Never knowing which star to steer by.
I'm saying to you now,
In the quiet of our locker room,
Before the play-offs,
And after our family tragedy,
We will chart our own course
Around the Sirens of Hype and Distraction,
All hands working together to
Sail our ship on a straight line
Through dangerous waters,
To return home to pour champagne
Into our trophy cup of champions.

Garrett James

Then,
In summer,

> I thought basketball
> Was a one-on-one game,
> Me, with the rock,
> Trying to get around
> The guys I played with in the park.

Now,
In winter,

> I think I'm
> Carrying the team,
> Me, with the rock,
> Trying to do what it takes for
> The guys I play with in the gym.

I dribble the ball for a whole lot of people:

> My mom, who needs a new place,
> My sister, who needs money for her education,
> My relatives, who wait for me to make millions,
> My coach, who always believes in me,
> My fans, who come to my every game.

Then,

> Basketball used to be fun.

Now,

> It seems more like a job.

Russell Granger, Town Mortician

Pile the bodies high at Sawmill Road and Highway 9.
Shovel them under and let me work—
      I am the mortician; I cover all.

And pile them high at Getty's Curve
And pile them high at Junction and Boot Road.
Shovel them under and let me work.
Two years, ten years, and tourists ask the townspeople:
      What happened to that bus?
      Where are the survivors now?

      I am the mortician.
      Let me work.

E. Z. Pratt

When I got kicked off the team,
I didn't think I could sink no lower.
I was wrong.
When I got kicked outta school,
I was told it would
"Be in your best interests
To pursue your education elsewhere"—
Fancy words for being thrown outta the game.
Now, instead of hittin' the boards,
I'm hittin' the bottle.
Instead of drainin' threes,
I'm drainin' long-necks.
Instead of floatin' down the lane,
I'm stumblin' in the streets.
Instead of throwin' down jams,
I'm just throwin' up.
I coulda been a hell of a ballplayer,
I could be playin' with the guys right now,
If I didn't screw up so bad.
Hey, man, pass me back my bottle.
It's the only kind of pass
I can handle these days.

Jason Cohen

Coach is always saying that
Adversity makes you stronger,
On and off the court.
But I wonder, is there sort of a
Law of diminishing returns on that?
I mean, isn't it truer
That a locker full of troubles
Just makes you angrier?
Take my friend, Darnell, for instance,
Whose home life really sucks.
I worry about him blowing up one day.
Yeah, he can come over to my house for dinner
As often as he likes.
Yeah, he could have a great game
Nearly every night.
Yeah, he could dream the pro dream
Each and every day.
But can all that
Change a crappy life
In a crappy neighborhood?
Man cannot live by dreams alone,
Can he?

Darnell Joyce

Everyone's tryin' to help me:
Coach, Ms. Chartoff, Jason,
Even Jason's grandmother.
But it's like workin' out in the weight room:
Nobody's gonna do the job for you at each station.
Nobody's gonna break out in a sweat for you.
Nobody's gonna lift the bar off your shoulders.
You just gotta find the strength
To work things out for yourself.
You gotta push, squeeze, lift, and stretch
To the best of your ability
And not worry 'bout
The resistance you're gonna meet every day.
Some people who know me might say,
"Darnell, you got a tough life, man,"
And they'd be right to say that,
But I ain't whinin' 'bout the way things are.
There's some a lot worse off than me.
In this life you gotta pull your own weight,
Alone, with nobody even spottin' you.

Niki Carmichael, School Broadcaster

TIME OUT, SCORE TIED AT 52. WINNER GOES UPSTATE, LOSER GOES HOME. THE AMBASSADORS OF CARTER HIGH, THE ONLY TEAM TO BEAT TOWER THIS YEAR, HAVE GIVEN THE TIGERS FITS ALL NIGHT. THEY HAVE DOUBLE-, EVEN TRIPLE-TEAMED JAMES, EFFECTIVELY SHUTTING DOWN THE TOWER OFFENSE. TEN SECONDS TO GO, TIGER BALL, EVERYONE IN THE BUILDING KNOWS WHO'S GETTING THE BALL. HERE WE GO, HOLD ON TO YOUR HATS:

:10   Tigers inbound, Padilla to James,
:08   James dribbles, Carter not wanting to foul,
:06   James near the top of the key,
:04   Pumps once, lets fly with a long jumper,
:02   Off the rim, a scramble for the ball,
:01   Joyce up with it, flings it toward the basket,
:00   Ball in the air . . . it's good, it's GOOD!

TIGERS WIN, TIGERS WIN, TIGERS WIN!

Basketball Pulse

Post up low,
Give and go,
Match up quick,
Set a pick,
Run the floor,
We want more,
Grab the ball,
Ref, bad call,
Sly back door,
Nestor's score,
Garrett's J,
Drop all day,
Tamba's jump,
We are pumped,
Joyce on high,
Flying by,
Stanton steals,
Mass appeal,
Game on line,
Overtime?
Crazy thing,
Wild fling,
Ball in air,
All eyes stare,
Ball falls through.
Win by two.

Roman Kirenova

Boris, Boris, she captured me,
Every part of me,
My heart, my soul,
And other parts
Too private to mention.
I don't know how it happened,
But I think it was right after we beat Carter.
People spilled out from stands, and
Center court became spaghetti-tangle of arms and legs.
I felt a hand on my arm, then on my leg,
Then on my butt.
My butt?
I looked around and saw Vonessa smiling.
"We won, we won, you big doofus,
Gimme a kiss," she screamed.
She kissed me like it was last kiss on earth,
Like she was trying to breathe life into me.
People must have thought
Basketball was on our minds,
Believe me, our attention was on stuff happening
A good deal lower.
Boris, Boris, she captured me,
Part by part,
But I don't mind,
A whole lot.

Holly Cooper, Hudson Flowers

Haven't seen you in a while.
You're right, I used to work at the inn.
But I always wanted to run a place of my own.
Yes, I heard about it.
Terrible, isn't it?
What were they doin' out on the road
In weather like this?
For a basketball game?
Silly, don't you think?
I sent a basket of flowers over to Russell.
No, the boys weren't from around here.
Doesn't make it any less sad
For their parents, does it?
The news is not all bad;
I hear a lot of them survived,
Thank God.
Now what can I do for you?
How about some nice geraniums?

Vonessa Leighton

Well, Daddy,
I found a new boyfriend.
A good man, just like you, Daddy,
Well, almost.
Yeah, he's on the team.
We were sort of thrown together,
Well, kinda.
I love bein' around him, Daddy,
I hope you get a chance to meet him,
Well, soon.
You thought I was callin' about basketball?
Love lasts a lot longer
Than a thirty-two-minute game,
Well, hopefully.
How's my little stepbrother doin'?
Sure wish you guys lived closer.
Talk to you next weekend.
My boyfriend?
He's light-skinned,
Very light-skinned.
You understand what I'm sayin'?
Well, Daddy?
I can't hear you clearly.
Does the static from your end
Interfere with the long distance connection
Between us?

E. Z. Pratt

After my family done thrown me out,
I had no choice but to come here.
"Three hots and a cot,"
That's what they call the shelter.
I ain't crazy, man,
But I will be,
If I stay here any longer.
I'll be just like the others,
Drinkin', smokin', talkin'
Out loud to nobody in particular.
Or worst of all,
I'll be listenin' to voices
Inside my head,
Talkin' to me.
I shoulda stayed in school, man,
Where there was always somethin' to do.
I gotta get outta this place,
Where there is nothin' to do,
'Cept watch out for the sickos
Who try to steal you blind.
Shelters don't shelter you from nothin', man.

yrone Porter

Hey, little bro,
My little Tiger man,
What's up?
You want my Tiger shirt?
You already got one.
You want a Tiger bumper sticker?
You're too young to drive a car.
You want my sneakers?
You'll swim around in 'em.
Oh, you were only playin'.
Do I wanna know what you really want?
No, not really.
Oh, I was only playin', too.
Go ahead, tell me.
You wanna know
If you can come upstate with us?
That you'll dress up as the official Tiger mascot?
That you'll be good and won't get sick on the bus?
Sure, I can ask Coach that.
Least I can do since you're my number-one fan.
No, later, I swear I'll ask him, I promise.
Yes, I'll ask him if you can come along for the ride.

Greg Hoskins, Coach

Before we board the bus to go upstate,
I'd like to take a moment
To thank the people
Who have made this a most successful season.
Win or lose, we are already victorious,
Given the loving support of family, friends, and fans.
I'd also like to thank the faculty and staff of Tower,
Who have cheered us through the good times and the bad.
Yes, we've had our share of adversity, on and off the court,
But we rallied 'round our school banner
To see our team handle itself with intelligence and grace.
Finally, I'd like to thank my wife, Mary Beth,
Who understands fully that my heart divides gently
Between my love for her and my love for the game.
See you soon, sweetie, hopefully with the championship trophy.
I have one more thing to say:
To those who say we should not go upstate
Because of the prospect of inclement weather,
I say we have come too far
Not to follow what fate has in store for us.
We have made the long march into March;
We cannot turn back now.
You will see, we will long remember this day,
Over
Time.

Dennis Carleton

Almost didn't make the bus.

Kept waiting for my pop to show.

Mom says the garage musta been busy.

I say the garage coulda been empty,

And he would have found an excuse not to come.

A part-time player don't interest him none, it seems.

Hey, Porter, get your skinny-ass brother offa me.

Who said he could come on the bus with us?

Coach?

As what?

Next you be tellin' me

The kid's gonna suit up and get some p.t.

I said keep him offa me.

I wanna look out the window

And see some snow that don't look like crap.

The trees up here be wearin' white coats.

It's mad beautiful.

I wish my pop could see all this.

OK, kid, you can sit next to me if you want.

At least you came to wish us luck.

Pop, does a full-time son interest you some?

On the bus to the state finals, I'm thinkin',
Who needs college?
I sure don't.
I could make the jump into the pros right now.
I could go high enough in the draft so that
I wouldn't ever have to worry about nothin'.
Who needs college?
I sure don't.
I could get my Mercedes now.
I could get my family outta the projects.
I could get my kid anything he wants.
But would I play or ride the pine?
Could I take the eighty-two-game schedule?
Should I give up college just for the money?
The pro life is something I always wanted,
Always dreamed about ever since I was little.
But am I giving up too much, too soon,
Fun for the big bucks,
College for the cover of *Sports Illustrated?*
Deep down, I don't know if I'm old enough
To make such an important decision.
Who needs college?
Maybe I do.
Then again, it's hard to turn down millions, ain't it?
But, hey, I got some time to decide all this.

Tamba Senesie

In my Nigeria,
There are but two seasons,
Wet and dry.
In the rainy season,
The skies open daily
And replenish the parched earth.
In the dry season,
The red clay dust covers the children
Selling oranges by the roadside.
Oh, I do miss the rain drumming softly
On the tin-covered roof of my grandfather's house.
I do miss, too, the cries of the brightly clad women
As they sell their wares on market day.
But is it not a marvel?
Here am I—an African,
Miles from home,
Riding in a coach bus,
Far from my school,
Playing a sport inside an arena,
While outside my bus window,
The snow settles softly on passing treetops.
I am so happy for the sights I have witnessed.
I am so happy for the experiences I have gained.
I thank Allah and America for all they have given me.
May I be worthy of their magnificent bounties.

Tyrone Porter

Hey, man,
You wanna speed up this bus?
Ain't you goin' kinda slow?
We got a game to catch, you know.
I can't wait;
It's a lock.
I'm gonna bring home that trophy
For my school, for my friends,
For you, my little brother,
But most of all, for me.
I'm gonna wear that championship ring
For the rest of my life
And never take it off.
I'm gonna wear it next to my wedding ring
And show it to my children and grandchildren.
Hey, man,
You wanna slow down this bus?
Ain't you goin' kinda fast?
We got plenty of time to get there, you know.

EPILOGUE

Dion Porter, Tyrone's Brother

Have you seen my brother, Tyrone?
He's a big, goofy-lookin' dude
With his hat on backwards
And fake eyeglasses
He sometimes uses
To make hisself look intellectual.
Hey, I'm all right.
Leave me alone.
Go take care of the other people.
I gotta go look for my brother.
Hey, we still gonna play the game,
Ain't we?
Everybody's gonna be OK,
Won't they?
We just gotta call a meeting,
Get everybody together,
And keep focused on what we gotta do.
We're gonna win.
You better believe it, and
My brother's gonna be a big star.
Hey, Mr. Trooper, you seen my brother?
Can you tell me where he is?
We gotta get ready for the game.

Hospital Report

Dennis Carleton ....serious

Jason Cohen..good

Garrett James ....serious, but stable

Darnell Joyce..good

Roman Kirenova..dead on arrival

Nestor Padilla...treated and released

Dion Porter...treated and released

Tyrone Porter...dead on arrival

Tamba Senesie...good

Tysheen Stanton ....dead on arrival

Coach Greg Hoskins ....critical

Vonessa Leighton...treated and released

Tony Grimaldi ....dead on arrival

Edith Fromer, Town Resident

In summer,
This is a Huck Finn pond,
Near the hill where the accident took place,
Dangling lines catching nothing
But the local gossip.
In winter,
This is a Hans Brinker pond,
Near the hill where the accident took place,
Flashing blades catching nothing
But the afternoon sun.
Now,
Ugly police tape
Has eliminated
Summer and winter
Forever.
Hope we don't get no more snow.
I'm looking forward to spring.

About the Author

Mel Glenn grew up in Brooklyn, New York, and has been teaching English for twenty-seven years at his alma mater, Lincoln High School. He and his wife, Elyse, live in Brooklyn with their two sons, Jonathan and Andrew.

Mr. Glenn is the author of six books of poetry for young adults and three novels. He has won many awards, including the Christopher Award, the American Library Association's Best Book of the Best Books, and the Golden Kite Honor.